Plants and Animals

Consulting Editor: Richard Hantula

GARETH**STEVENS**
GS PUBLISHING
A Member of the WRC Media Family of Companies

Please visit our web site at: www.garethstevens.com
For a free color catalog describing Gareth Stevens Publishing's
list of high-quality books and multimedia programs,
call 1-800-542-2595 (USA) or 1-800-387-3178 (Canada).
Gareth Stevens Publishing's fax: (414) 332-3567.

Library of Congress Cataloging-in-Publication Data

Plants and animals. — North American ed.
    p. cm. — (Real world science)
  Includes index.
  ISBN 0-8368-6308-9 (lib. bdg.)
  1. Biology—Juvenile literature. I. Series.
QH309.2.P53   2006
570—dc22   2005054147

This North American edition first published in 2006 by
Gareth Stevens Publishing
A Member of the WRC Media Family of Companies
330 West Olive Street, Suite 100
Milwaukee, WI 53212 USA

Editor: Kate Latham
Inside design: Rachel Clark
Illustrators: Phil Ford & Stephen Dew
Educational Consultant: John Stringer BSc
Gareth Stevens editor: Leifa Butrick
Gareth Stevens art direction: Tammy West
Gareth Stevens cover design: Dave Kowalski
Gareth Stevens production: Jessica Morris & Robert Kraus

Picture credits: © Digital Vision: cover; Bruce Coleman Collections 10b, 12, 23, /E & P Bauer 8,
/E Bjurstrom 27, /Jane Burton 16, /Alain Compost 20, /Sarah Cook 29, /Christer Fredriksson 24, /Hans
Reinhard 4, /Peter Zabransky 15, /Gunter Ziesler 7, 19; Sidney Francis 10t; Science Photo Library 26.

Printed in the United States of America

1 2 3 4 5 6 7 8 9 10 09 08 07 06

Contents

Being Alive

Have you ever wondered whether life exists on other planets? Well, until humans go to pay a visit to them or aliens arrive here, you won't know. What you can be certain of, however, is that our planet – Earth – is home to a fabulous variety of living things, from the tiniest bacteria (which can be seen only through powerful microscopes) to huge blue whales, which can grow as long as 100 feet (30 meters) – longer than a swimming pool.

What makes something alive?

Scientists have identified and named about 1.8 million different species – or types – of living things, but there are probably many millions more out there that we have yet to discover. Every living thing is made up of tiny "cells" that work together to form the physical body and to carry out the necessary functions of life. You are made of trillions of these cells, not counting the trillions of bacteria that live on your skin and inside your body.

Giant sequoia trees are the largest living things on Earth. They can be up to 300 feet (90 m) high and 30 feet (9 m) wide.

Changing world

Most scientists believe that life first appeared on Earth about 3.8 billion years ago, when the planet was already about 800 million years old and still cooling down from the process that made it. The first organisms, or living things, may have been something like bacteria. Gradually, more and more complex organisms appeared. This constant change over time is called evolution, and it's the way that most scientists think life on Earth developed. Evolution means that species change as they adapt to different conditions. Those that cannot adapt die out. They become extinct.

An amoeba is a very simple life-form that lives in water. It is a protist – an organism that consists of only one cell.

The nucleus is the "brain" of the cell, controlling its functions.

What's in a name?

In the eighteenth century, Swedish scientist Carolus Linnaeus (1707–1778) realized that, with all the many different types of animals and plants in the world, there was an urgent need for a method of classifying them, that is, for putting them into some sort of order based on how closely related they were.

He worked out a way of naming them so that every species of living thing would have a name that people would recognize. Each species was given a two-word name in Latin. His system was a great improvement because some animals had

Species – a group of organisms that can breed together

Genus – a group of species that have many common features

names made up of more than ten words! The first name showed the group of animals – known as the genus – that the species belonged to (a bit like your family name), while the second name showed the actual species (like your first name). This system is still used by scientists today. Tigers and lions, for example, both belong to the same genus, *Panthera*. But the lion is *Panthera* (genus) *leo* (species), while the tiger is *Panthera tigris*. You, by the way, are formally known as *Homo sapiens* (provided that you are human, of course).

TRY THIS

Grouping together

You will need a collection of coins. Now pick out features – such as the size, shape, and color – that make some different from others. This is just what Linnaeus would have done when classifying species. Draw up a chart, like a family tree, to divide your coins into groups, where all coins look alike in some way.

You could also try this with a selection of leaves from a park. They could be grouped by features such as color and size.

Amazing Fact

Tardigrades, or water bears, are tiny animals that live in places such as among damp leaves in woody areas or in gutters of houses. They can "play dead" for as long as twenty-five years, and then, if placed in water, immediately come back to life. This amazing ability helps them survive times when their normally wet home is dried out.

Living Places

You could probably describe the sort of area you live in and its surroundings. Are the stores easy to get to? Is there a park nearby? Does the Sun shine a lot, or does it rain all the time? Since living things are found just about everywhere on Earth's surface (and beneath it), their surroundings vary a lot, but they are able to survive only in places, or "habitats," that provide the food and shelter they need.

Plants and animals survive in environments that vary widely in terms of climate, conditions, and resources. They must adapt to cope with their surroundings and to protect themselves.

Habitat scrapbook

Search through magazines to find pictures of as many different habitats as you can, if possible showing the types of plants and animals found there. Cut the pictures out (get permission first), and use them to make a habitat scrapbook in which you can see the world's living places at a glance. Notice the similarities between animals that live in the same types of habitat but in different places, such as the monkeys that live in South America's tropical forests and those that live in the forests of Africa.

Species of animals and plants can naturally die out (become extinct). Many scientists think that the speed at which this is happening has increased because of human beings. As the human population increases (there are now more than 6 billion people in the world and roughly 250 babies are born every minute), we are using up more resources, destroying more habitats, causing more pollution, and changing the climate. Now thousands of animals are threatened. These include well-known species such as the tiger, panda, and gorilla, and many smaller animals that might disappear without us noticing. Plants are threatened as well, and this endangers the animals that rely on them for food, and also us, because humans use many plants as cures for illness and disease.

The tiger could die out in five years' time in some areas if it is not protected from poachers and loss of habitat.

African grasslands

No animal lives in isolation; all are linked together. This is true everywhere in the world. For example, look at the dry grasslands of the African savanna. These extremely spacious grasslands are warm all year-round, with a dry season during the summer. The soil is too poor for many trees to grow there, but grasses and small bushes can survive. Some animals there eat just plants (herbivores). They feed most of the day because there isn't much nourishment in grasses and leaves. Zebras eat the tough top parts of grasses while giraffes, with their long necks, can eat from the few trees. This means that they don't compete for food and can survive together. Herbivores are tasty meals for the meat eaters (carnivores), such as lions and hyenas.

Amazing Fact

The arctic fox is a great survivor. It can withstand freezing conditions in ice and snow where the temperature may fall as low as –60°F (–50°C). A thick layer of fat under its skin and very thick fur help keep out the cold.

Many species of animals live on the African savanna grasslands.

Who Eats What?

People worldwide depend on the family and friends around them, especially nearby neighbors. Animals and plants that live in a particular place or habitat are also linked together – often because they eat each other to survive. Humans who live in the same place talk of being part of a community. Animals and plants that share the same habitat also form a community.

Owls feed on a wide range of animals, including insects, fish, small birds, and mammals, including young foxes.

Down the chain and through the web

The way that a community interacts with its surroundings – whether they are a grassland or a swamp – forms a relationship called an ecosystem. Essential to the whole operation is the Sun. Sunlight energy flows down to Earth, into plants (which use it to make food, as explained on page 12), and then into the animals that eat the plants, and on into the animals that eat those animals, and so on.

The easiest way to describe a who-eats-what relationship is by using what is called a food chain.

Take a mouse and a snake. The mouse feeds on grass, and the snake eats mice. The energy from the Sun flows along the chain from grass to snake. Simple? It's not quite as simple as that. In woodlands, mice eat grass, but they are also hunted by large birds, which might also kill a rabbit (which also eats grass). Foxes also eat mice, and so on. Suddenly, the simple food chain has hundreds of links and has become a food web. This is the easiest way to show how a community forms an ecosystem.

Energy from the Sun passes from plants to herbivores and small animals, and then to larger animals in the food chain.

Where did it come from?

You will need a pen and paper. Every time you eat something, you find yourself at the end of a food chain. Unless you get eaten by a whale or a lion, of course, in which case you're the second-to-last link in the chain! Make a list of all the foods you have eaten today, and then try to work out the food chain that led to you. For example, a piece of beef comes from a cow that fed on grass that made its own food using sunlight. The cereal that you had for breakfast may have been made from wheat or oats, which are plants and which use sunlight energy to make food, as do vegetables and fruit. Even chocolate comes from a plant – the cocoa plant.

Amazing Fact

In the depths of the ocean, as much as 8,000 feet (2,500 m) or more below the surface, it is pitch-black, and the water pressure is so high that it would squash you as flat as a pancake. Living things are found here, however, including giant tube worms up to 10 feet (3 m) long. They live around vents, like chimneys, from which hot water gushes, heated by rocks in Earth's crust. With no sunlight, food chains here are very different from the surface. The hot water contains sulfur. This is used as an energy source by tiny bacteria that then provide food for the tube worms.

Did You Know?

Not all plants and animals are eaten by other species as food. Dead animals and plants that haven't been eaten are cleaned up by very useful organisms known as decomposers. These species (which aren't actually classified as plants or animals) are the fungi and bacteria that live in the soil and break down dead living things so that they seem to disappear. What actually happens is that they release special minerals, such as nitrogen and phosphorus, into the soil. These are soaked up through plant roots and help plants grow and prosper, along with the animals that eat the plants, until they eventually die and are recycled once again by the decomposers.

Plant Life

Plants will grow wherever there is water and light and it is not too cold and windy. Below ground, their roots take in water from the soil. The water travels up the stem to other parts of the plant. Water helps plants stand straight up, as you may notice if your houseplants are not given the water they need. What you may not realize is that without plants, we humans and all other animals would not survive. Plants are the source of the oxygen in the air, the stuff we need to breathe to stay alive. So, be nice to plants!

Flowering plants

The best-known plants are probably plants with flowers, also known as flowering plants. They're the kinds of plants you find in the garden, or at a florist, or even in a field of wheat. (Yes, wheat has flowers as well, but not very colorful ones.) While a plant's green leaves use sunlight to make food, the flowers produce seeds that will eventually grow into new plants. The plant's roots dig downward, into the ground, to keep the plant standing straight. Roots also absorb water and minerals from the soil that are necessary for the plant to make its own food and keep healthy.

A flowering plant, with a single flower head at the top of the stem.

Did You Know?

Trees that lose their leaves every autumn are called deciduous trees. The leaves often turn bright colors before they separate from their branch and fall to the ground. It is too cold in winter for the leaves to make any food, so the tree loses its leaves for the winter months and makes new ones the following spring.

Plants without flowers

There are other types of plants as well. Mosses are tiny plants that generally live in clumps in wet places. Ferns are bigger, but they also usually like damp places. Mosses and ferns don't make seeds. They reproduce by releasing tiny spores. Unlike seeds, which tend to contain a bit of food to give the new plant a start, spores usually consist of a single cell with little or no food. A spore will grow into a new plant only if it lands in the right place.

Yet another type consists of the big conifers, including pine trees and your Christmas tree. Conifers produce seeds, but not inside flowers. They make seeds in cones. Many conifers have very narrow leaves that look like needles. In fact, that's what their leaves are called. Most conifers don't lose their leaves all at once in autumn. This helps them survive in places that can be dry or very cold.

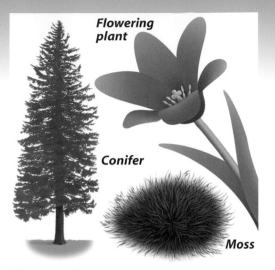

Flowering plant

Conifer

Moss

Mosses first appeared over 400 million years ago, followed by conifers millions of years later. Flowering plants developed a little over 100 million years ago.

Amazing Fact

Flowering plants form the biggest and most varied group of plants on Earth. There are some 260,000 different species found everywhere from baking deserts to the freezing Arctic.

TRY THIS

Water flow

You will need a jar or glass, some colored ink or food coloring, and a stick of leafy celery. Water moves up a plant's stem along tiny tubes called xylem, which are a bit like drainpipes. To see how this happens, take a stick of celery and ask an adult to trim one end. Put the stem in a jar containing a mixture of ink (or food coloring) and water at least 2 inches (5 centimeters) deep. Leave it in sunlight for twelve hours. Now, take the celery out of the jar and ask an adult to cut the celery stick in two at its midpoint. Look at the cut ends. You will see lots of colored dots (the color of the ink that you used). These show where the xylem tubes – carrying the colored water – have been cut in half.

Food from the Sun

Plants can't move, so they can't go looking for food, but they don't have to. They can make their own food without going to the trouble of chasing after prey or going to the supermarket. All it takes is a basic recipe and a few simple ingredients.

Green is good

Food making happens inside a plant's leaves. Inside each leaf are lots of tiny oval blobs called chloroplasts. Packed inside each of these is a green substance called chlorophyll. Chlorophyll is remarkable because it can actually grab hold of the energy in sunlight and make use of it. Two other ingredients are needed for the plant to make food: the gas carbon dioxide (which comes from the air through tiny holes in the leaves) and water, which comes up to the leaves through the stem from the roots. The plant's recipe uses a process called photosynthesis, in which the energy trapped by chlorophyll joins together carbon dioxide and water to produce a sugar called glucose. This is packed full of energy that the plant can use. You make use of it too – every time you eat a banana or any other part of a plant.

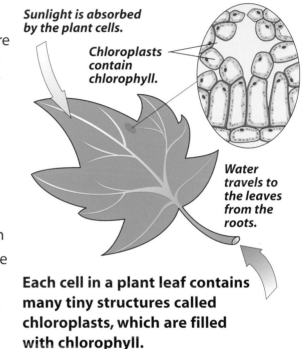

Sunlight is absorbed by the plant cells.

Chloroplasts contain chlorophyll.

Water travels to the leaves from the roots.

Each cell in a plant leaf contains many tiny structures called chloroplasts, which are filled with chlorophyll.

Tropical forests

The world's tropical forests lie in a belt around the equator, from Central and South America, through Africa, to Southeast Asia. If you were standing in one now, you would be hot and sweating, and you might find a few bugs running up your leg. The mixture of plenty of sunshine, lots of warmth, and water makes a tropical forest ideal for plant growth. Many different types of plants in the forest provide homes and food to millions of animal species. Unfortunately, all around the world these forests are at risk of being destroyed. As human populations grow, people want to chop down the trees, either to make money from timber or to create new farmland.

Plant gas

You will need a big bowl, a glass or beaker, and some pondweed. Fill the bowl with water. Put the pondweed in the glass and then fill the glass with water, right to the top. Place the glass carefully in the bowl of water and then turn the glass upside down. Be sure it's still full of water and that its open end rests on the bottom of the bowl. Make sure there is no air in the glass. Place the bowl in sunlight and leave it for a few hours. You will soon notice bubbles of gas appearing on the pondweed leaves. In time, these float up to the top of the glass. This is the oxygen that plants produce when they make food for themselves.

Did You Know?

Hundreds of years ago, people believed that there were man-eating plants. Fortunately, that's not true, but there are some plants – called carnivorous plants – that gobble up juicy flies and other small creatures. The Venus flytrap has a particularly nasty surprise waiting for its victims. It has special leaves that work like a spring trap. If a fly lands on the trap, the two halves of the trap snap shut. No amount of struggling can free the poor fly. Pretty soon the Venus flytrap digests the fly, feasting on its nutritious juices.

Following the Sun

Plants grow toward the Sun, and you can test this. You will need two small bowls or half eggshells, a couple of handfuls of seed compost or a similar seed-starting mix, a packet of flower seeds, and a box with a small slit in one side (get an adult to help you with this). Take the bowls or half eggshells. Fill each with seed compost. Sprinkle some flower seeds over the compost in each one, and water them carefully. Put one set of seeds in a dark place, such as a cupboard. Cover the other seeds with the box with the slit in the side; Turn the box so that the slit faces toward a source of sunlight. Leave the bowls for a week to let the seeds sprout. What do you discover? The seeds left in the dark have grown into plants that are long and skinny with yellowish leaves. They have been struggling to find the light they need to grow. The ones under the box have green leaves and have grown toward the slit in the box in an effort to get out into the sunlight.

Seeds and Growth

How many poor, defenseless baby plants have you eaten recently? None at all, you may answer, shocked by the thought. Think again. If you have eaten peanuts, peas, beans, rice, lentils, or popcorn, baby plants are precisely what have gone into your mouth. All of those foods are seeds, and seeds are created by plants when they reproduce.

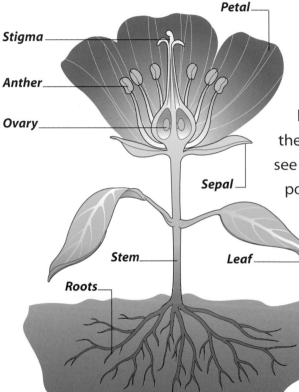

Petal
Stigma
Anther
Ovary
Sepal
Stem
Leaf
Roots

Seeds

Seeds are made by flowers. If you were to take a flower such as a lily or tulip and slice it in half lengthwise, it would look something like the flower shown at left. You can see the brightly colored petals that attract insects. You can also see the anthers that produce and are covered by powdery pollen, one or more sticky stigmas that pick up pollen, and the ovary where the seeds develop. Pollen gets shifted from the anther of one flower to the stigma of another by insects visiting to feed on the sweet nectar produced by flowers, and sometimes also by the wind. The pollen fertilizes the eggs inside the flower's ovary, and soon the ovary – now called a fruit – is bulging with seeds. Each seed is a package containing a baby plant and the food store that will keep it going as it germinates (grows).

How does your garden grow?

Whether they're lilies, oak trees, cabbages, or carrots, most of the plants around you grow from seeds. With a bit of luck, if a seed lands on a decent bit of soil, it has a good chance of germinating – that is, growing into a new plant. It also needs a reasonable amount of warmth – it won't germinate on a freezing winter day – and plenty of water. The new plant's stem grows up toward the Sun while its roots dig downward into the soil in search of water. Very soon, if it isn't eaten by a passing rabbit or squashed by your boot, it will produce flowers and seeds of its own.

Watching germination

You will need a clean jar or tall glass, two sheets of blotting paper or paper towel, cotton, and a broad (fava) bean seed or similar seed. Normally you can't see germination happening, because the seed is buried in the soil. This way you can. Take the jar or glass and line it with the blotting paper or paper towel. Loosely fill the inside of the blotting paper with cotton. Now put the bean seed halfway down the jar, between the paper and the glass. Add some water to the cotton, but do not cover the seed. Put the jar in a dark place (to pretend the seed is underground) and look at it every day. Add water when necessary. At first the seed swells as it takes in water. Then the seed splits, and a root pops out and grows downward. A shoot soon appears and grows upward, reaching for the Sun. In a few days, the first leaves appear, and you can leave the jar in sunlight. Having used the food stored in the seed, the young plant can now make its own food using sunlight.

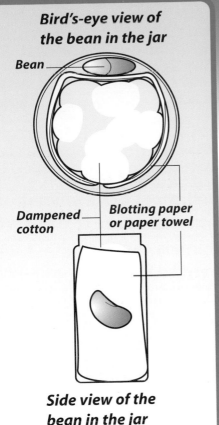

Bird's-eye view of the bean in the jar

Bean

Dampened cotton

Blotting paper or paper towel

Side view of the bean in the jar

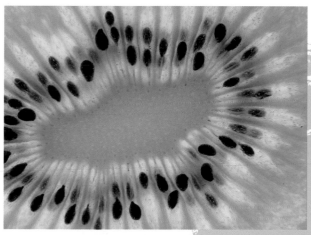

The seeds inside a kiwi fruit.

Did You Know?

Plants have many clever ways of dispersing or spreading their seeds. If seeds landed too close to their parent, in no time they would be slurping up the parent's water supply. Strawberries and similar fruits are yummy; animals wolf them down, and the seeds come out the animal's other end unharmed and nowhere near the parent. Maple trees have wing-shaped fruits that spin through the air. Dandelions produce tiny parachutes that simply blow away. Coconuts fall into the sea and wash up on another beach. Some fruits are sticky or hooked. They get caught in animals' fur and spread that way.

Flower power

You will need a flower, a small sharp knife, and a magnifying glass. With an adult's help, slice the flower carefully along its length. Look at the petals, the anthers, the sticky stigma, and the ovary with the magnifying glass. Try the same thing with a piece of fruit, such as an apple. In the center are the seeds, surrounded by the fleshy fruit.

15

Animal Life

What do fluffy rabbits, scary snakes, and biting fleas have in common? They're all animals, and so are we. What makes an animal an animal and not a plant? Well, most of us animals move around and don't sit in the same place all the time like a tree (except when we're watching TV). We all eat things, and most animals can see what's happening around them – a great advantage if you want to find food and avoid nasty surprises.

Millions and millions

If you went for a swim and met a blue whale, you would never forget it. It is twenty-five times longer than you. If a tiny plankton animal floated past, you would totally ignore it, not because you are rude, but because it is too small to see. Between the biggest and the smallest, there is a huge amount of animal life to be seen. Scientists have identified and named over one and one-half million different species of animals, but this is only part of the story. No one knows how many species of animals remain to be discovered. There may be 30, 50, or even an incredible 100 million. So you'd better start looking. They might name a new species after you!

Chameleons change color in response to factors such as temperature and light and emotions such as fright.

Did You Know?

It's a dangerous world out there. There are plenty of hungry predators just waiting to pounce and sink their teeth into passing prey. So it's hardly surprising that animals try to defend themselves. Here are some of the ways they do it:

▶▶ **Hide.** If you blend in with your surroundings, no one can see you – in theory. The chameleon, for example, sometimes actually changes color.

▶▶ **Run.** This is what you would probably do to escape the toothy attentions of a passing crocodile or lion, but you wouldn't be able to catch a high-speed hare or overtake an ostrich.

▶▶ **Disable the predator.** Two tiny "bags" in the skunk's bottom work just like water pistols. They squirt a stinking, stinging liquid into an attacker's face, leaving the opponent temporarily blinded and very, very smelly.

Is there life in soil?

You will need a small glass jar, a plastic funnel, a flexible desktop task lamp, a handful of garden soil, and a magnifying glass. Garden soil may look pretty dull and lifeless, but it is actually teeming with tiny animals. To see some of them, put the funnel in the top of the jar and the soil in the funnel. Position the lamp so that its bulb is 1 foot (30 centimeters) above the funnel. Switch the lamp on and leave it there for about an hour. Any animals in the soil will escape downward, away from the heat and light, into the jar. Now, tip the contents of the jar into a glass dish. Look at it with the magnifying glass. Notice how many different types of animals there are. (Be sure to return them safely back to the soil.)

Vertebrates and invertebrates

The animals we know about fall into two clear groups called vertebrates and invertebrates. To join the vertebrate club you need to have a backbone and a skeleton inside you. Members include fish, amphibians, reptiles, birds, and mammals. You may be surprised to know that most species don't have a backbone. This group is called invertebrates, and members include sea anemones, which stay fixed in one place and catch anything that floats past with their tentacles; earthworms, which stretch and shorten to push their way through the soil; and insects, such as beetles, which have hard, outside skeletons.

Amazing Fact

Damp, dark, and spooky caves are home to all sorts of strange and wonderful animals that never see the Sun. One of the oddest is the olm. This distant cousin of the frog doesn't need to see, because it lives in total darkness. It doesn't need to have an attractive pattern on its skin, either, because other olms can't see it!

Bones and Muscles

Tent poles are really useful. They make a framework to drape the tent fabric on, so there's space inside to move around in, and the tent doesn't fall down in the middle of the night. Bones do the same thing for an animal's body. The bony skeleton supports the body as well as protecting delicate parts inside like the brain and lungs.

Muscle man

Stretched between the bones are muscles that give the body its basic shape and allow movement – making it possible to run and jump, for example. Muscles are unique. They are the only body tissues that can contract (get shorter) to pull bones and make the body move. Muscles can only pull, not push, so they are normally arranged in pairs.

Moving around

How many different ways can you move? Most people can walk and run, just like lizards and leopards can (although sometimes we get out of breath). We can swim, but not with the same speed or style as a seal or a shark. To fly, we need planes, unlike birds, bats, and insects. When it comes to hopping, we just can't keep up with frogs or kangaroos. As for sliding, it's best to leave that to snakes and slugs. The point is that animals move in many different ways. From eels to elephants, animals generally move for the same reasons: to find food, avoid enemies (and relatives that turn up unexpectedly), and find a mate.

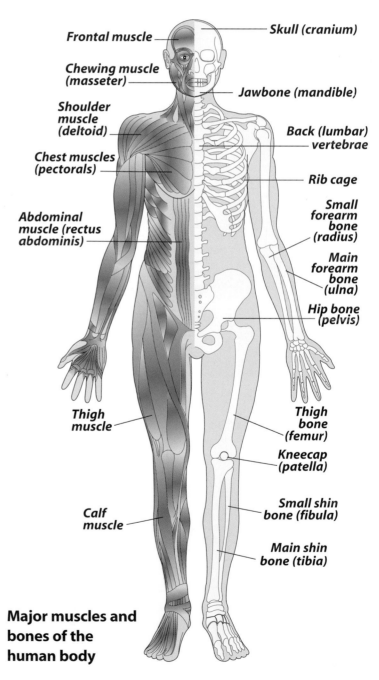

Frontal muscle

Skull (cranium)

Chewing muscle (masseter)

Jawbone (mandible)

Shoulder muscle (deltoid)

Back (lumbar) vertebrae

Chest muscles (pectorals)

Rib cage

Small forearm bone (radius)

Abdominal muscle (rectus abdominis)

Main forearm bone (ulna)

Hip bone (pelvis)

Thigh muscle

Thigh bone (femur)

Kneecap (patella)

Small shin bone (fibula)

Calf muscle

Main shin bone (tibia)

Major muscles and bones of the human body

A snail's pace

You will need a garden snail and a piece of glass or a glass plate. Find out how snails are able to move without the benefit of having legs. Put the snail on the glass. Wait until its head and foot (the flat part that it moves on) appear, then look at the animal from underneath. You will be able to see rhythmic ridges ripple down the foot from front to back. These are made by contractions of muscles in the foot, and they push the animal slowly forward – at a snail's pace, of course.

Did You Know?

Some animals make an annual journey – called migration – to breed, feed, or escape the winter cold. The amazing arctic tern is a bird that makes a migratory round trip of 20,000 miles (32,000 kilometers) each year. It breeds in the Arctic in the summer, then flies south to the Antarctic to make the most of the southern hemisphere summer, then returns to the Arctic. Gray whales travel 11,000 miles (18,000 km) each year when they move from feeding areas in the Arctic to warmer breeding grounds off California – a three months' journey – before returning to the Arctic.

Measuring muscles

You will need a tape measure. To see how two muscles work in opposite ways, roll up your sleeve and straighten your arm. Wrap the tape measure around your upper arm, and make a note of the measurement. Now bend your arm, and measure again. You will find the size of your upper arm has increased. This is because the biceps muscle at the front of the upper arm gets fatter and shorter as it contracts to bend your arm. Now straighten your arm. You will feel the muscle at the back of your arm tighten slightly. This is the triceps muscle, which straightens your arm. It does not bulge out as much as the biceps.

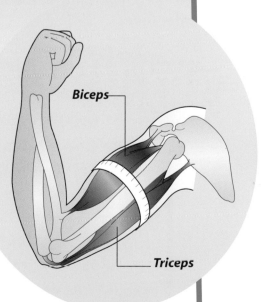

Biceps

Triceps

Brains and Behavior

Sometimes people call others "brainless," but they don't mean it literally. A person who really didn't have a brain wouldn't be able to feel, move, see, or have a personality. Sitting snugly protected inside the skull, the brain controls just about everything that goes on inside the body.

Meerkats are intelligent social animals. They live in communities, sharing duties such as watching for predators and hunting for food.

Brain power

Your brain is pinkish-gray and weighs about 3 pounds (1.5 kilograms). It receives a constant stream of information from your eyes, ears, skin, nose, and tongue to tell it what is happening outside the body. It sorts out all these messages and compares them to earlier experiences. Then it sends out instructions, often to your muscles, telling them to move the body, but also to other body parts. When you see a car racing toward you, your brain acts immediately, and you jump out of the way. This is called behavior. Making you feel sad, happy, angry, tired, or hungry is also part of the brain's job. It makes you unique: there's no one quite like you.

TRY THIS

Measuring reaction time

You will need a stopwatch (or any watch that shows seconds) and six other people. This experiment allows you to find out how long it takes a person to react to something. Ask the six people to stand in a line, hold hands, and close their eyes. Tell them that when they feel their hand squeezed, they should immediately squeeze the hand of the next person in line. The last person should shout when his or her hand is squeezed. Begin the experiment by squeezing the hand of the first person and starting the stopwatch at the same time. Stop the watch as soon as you hear the last person's shout. Write down the number of seconds from start to finish, and divide the number by six. That will tell how long, on average, it takes one person to react to something.

Rapid reflexes

Reflex actions happen quickly without you noticing. Often they protect you from danger – such as when your hand automatically pulls away from something sharp or hot. Try this one out on a friend standing in front of you. Look at your friend's eyes. Without warning, clap your hands in front of your friend's face. (Be careful not to touch it.) Your friend will immediately blink. Why? Because when something unusual happens in front of the eyes, the eyelids close by reflex to keep anything from harming the eyes.

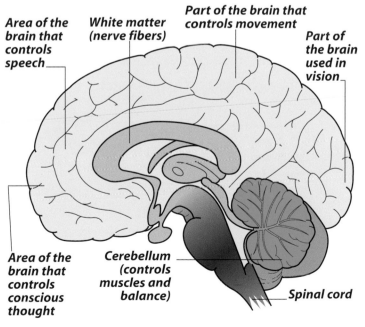

Area of the brain that controls speech

White matter (nerve fibers)

Part of the brain that controls movement

Part of the brain used in vision

Area of the brain that controls conscious thought

Cerebellum (controls muscles and balance)

Spinal cord

The inside of the human brain

Changing personality

One way in which scientists can find out about how brains work is by studying people whose brains have been damaged. The grisly case of the railroad construction worker Phineas Gage (1823–1860) is a classic example. One day in 1848, Gage, then working in Vermont, set a charge to blow up some rocks. A spark caused the explosion to occur too soon, and it drove an iron rod into his cheek, through the front part of his brain, and out the top of his head. Luckily, Gage survived, but he was a changed man. Before the accident, Gage had been kind, polite, and hardworking.

After the accident he was bad-tempered and unreliable. Gage's misfortune made scientists realize for the first time that our personalities are at least partly controlled by the front part of the brain.

Making Sense

How dangerous life would be if you couldn't see where you were going, or if your house caught fire and you couldn't smell the smoke. How boring it would be if you couldn't hear your stereo, or if foods such as chocolate and peaches had no taste. How strange it would seem if you couldn't feel heat or cold. You wouldn't feel a need to put on a coat when you go out into the snow. Using the senses is a necessary part of survival for all animals.

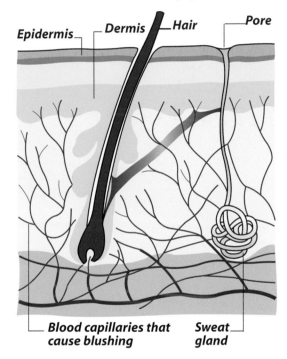

Epidermis — *Dermis* — *Hair* — *Pore*

Blood capillaries that cause blushing   *Sweat gland*

In touch

A living overcoat sounds a little creepy, but the skin on your body really is like a protective coat. It's waterproof to keep out water, and it's germproof to stop nasty bugs from getting in. As the diagram at left shows, the skin has an upper layer, called the epidermis, and a lower layer, the dermis. The epidermis is the main protective part. It gets darker when exposed to sunlight, in order to prevent harmful rays from reaching the dermis, where many blood vessels and nerves are located, along with such other structures as hair roots and sweat glands. The skin has a fantastic collection of sensors for touch, pressure, pain, heat, and cold. Because of them, you feel it when you are squashed on a bus or stand on a nail.

Seeing is believing

To find your favorite food, check out the latest fashions, or watch a movie, you need eyes. Your eyes are light detectors. Whenever light hits them – which is all the time when they are open – they send messages to the back of the brain. Just like doing a jigsaw puzzle, your brain puts all the bits of information together so you actually "see" whatever you're looking at.

Did You Know?

For some animals, the sense of smell is of vital importance. With a nose many times more sensitive than ours, dogs live in a world of smells far beyond human reach. Take a dog for a walk, and it will sniff everything in sight from tree trunks to doggy bottoms to get a full "smell picture" of its surroundings. Humans take advantage of this canine ability, using dogs to follow a criminal's scent and to find drugs and explosives at airports.

Sound detectors

What do you and elephants have, but sharks and rattlesnakes don't? The answer is ears. Ears are great for listening for the rustling sounds made by food on the move, as well as for the terrifying approach of a hungry enemy.

If you drop a stone in water, you will see ripples move outward from it. Sound waves travel though the air in much the same way. If you daydream in class and your teacher shouts at you, your teacher's vibrating vocal cords send pressure waves through the air to be picked up by your ears.

Elephants use their ears not only for hearing but also to regulate their body temperature.

Aromas and flavors

Smell and taste are really useful senses. They work together to let you enjoy the flavors of food and drinks. How do taste and smell actually work? Both depend on sensors that can detect chemicals. On your tongue there are lots of small bumps called papillae. These carry tiny sensors called taste buds. As for smell, it depends on a patch of smell sensors high above the nostrils in the nasal passages (where no finger can reach). These sensors pick up chemicals floating by in the air that you breathe in.

Automatic pupils

Small pupil in bright light

You will need a hand mirror. Use the mirror to look at your eyes. In the middle of each eye is a black dot called the pupil. This is actually a hole that lets light into the eye. Now go somewhere where the light is dim, but it's not completely dark. Your pupils will get bigger, or

Dilated pupil in dim light

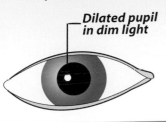

"dilated," to let in as much light as possible. Now go somewhere bright. The pupils will get smaller to keep the bright light from damaging your eyes. Your pupils get bigger and smaller automatically, without you having to think about it.

Food

As you've already seen, plants can make their own food by just sitting in the sunlight. They don't need to make a trip to the supermarket. Unfortunately you can't make your own food. Even if you go on a beach vacation for two weeks, you can't stop eating. You and other animals have to actively find food and eat it in order to get energy and grow. Luckily, animals feed on all sorts of things and feed in different ways, so we are not all competing for the same thing.

Some herbivores live in groups so that they can feed and watch for danger at the same time.

Meat and plants

Animals that just eat plants – such as cows, zebras, and grasshoppers – are known as herbivores. Wolves, sharks, polar bears, and other carnivores, or meat eaters, need a nice piece of meat to keep them going. Animals that are omnivores – such as humans, grizzly bears, and pigs – will eat anything that is put in front of them.

Food processing

Close your eyes and think about your favorite food. Imagine you are popping it into your mouth and enjoying its great flavor. Food's greatest value to you, however, comes after that. Something happens to your food when your body starts digesting, or processing, it. This occurs automatically. The only clues you may receive as to what's happening to the food are a few burps and rumbles, but what is really going on?

Snakes and other ectotherms, or "cold-blooded animals," do not have to eat every day, unlike endotherms, or "warm-blooded animals," such as dogs and humans. Ectotherms need far less energy from their food because they do not have to keep their bodies warm like we do. In fact, a dog needs so much energy that it has to eat ten times more than a snake of the same weight. Snakes may eat a large meal at one sitting, and then not eat again for weeks. (Imagine swallowing whole a hamburger twice your size.) The downside for snakes, and other reptiles, is that they need to spend time basking in the sun to warm up their bodies before they become fully active. Some humans also like to bask, but only to get a suntan.

Top to bottom

The human digestive system is a long tube running from the mouth (the tube's top opening) to the anus (bottom opening). It is up to 30 feet (9 m) long. Fortunately, the longest parts – the intestines – are curled up. Otherwise, you would need to be as tall as a house! Food gives you energy and the raw materials for growth. It is made up largely of big molecules that your body cannot use directly; the digestive system breaks down food into tiny molecules that the body can use. Crushed by the teeth, churned by the stomach, and attacked by chemical digesters called enzymes, food is reduced to the consistency of lumpy chicken soup. Useful stuff is soaked up through the intestines and into the bloodstream. Any leftover waste is dried out in the large intestine, where it picks up a brown color from waste blood cells and gets a distinctive smell from the bacteria that live there. It's quite an amazing process.

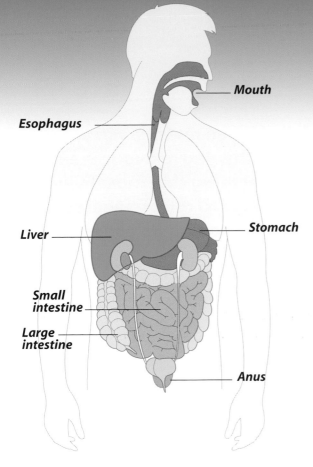

Mouth

Esophagus

Liver

Stomach

Small intestine

Large intestine

Anus

The human digestive system

Teeth

You will need a hand mirror. With your mouth open, hold the mirror so that you can see your teeth. Humans have four types of teeth, which make up a sort of digestive tool kit. Chisel-like incisor teeth at the front of the jaws cut food. Pointed canine teeth (longer in Dracula and other vampires) grip and pierce food. Flat premolars and molars at the back of the jaws grind and crush food. You have two sets of teeth during your lifetime. The first set – called the milk teeth or baby teeth – starts appearing at about the age of six months, usually causing sore gums and loud crying. Eventually, twenty milk teeth pop up through the gums. From about the age of six, they are gradually replaced by the second set – the permanent teeth – which grow up from below. By the age of eighteen or twenty, you will have thirty-two teeth in place (if you avoid fighting or falling out of trees). Count how many teeth you have.

Incisor

Canine

Premolar

Molar

25

The Breath of Life

It doesn't matter whether you're a human or a hawk, an owl or a pussy cat, an ox or a parrot. Once you stop breathing permanently, you're dead. Breathing gets air into the body, and the oxygen in air is something that most living things need in order to stay alive. Oxygen is essential to release energy locked in the food. Energy powers everything from owls swooping on prey to humans running for the bus.

Lungs

In the case of humans and our relatives (other vertebrates, not just aunts and uncles), breathing moves air in and out of the baglike lungs in the chest. From there, oxygen goes into the blood, which carries it to every single energy-hungry cell. A poisonous waste gas called carbon dioxide released by cells is carried back to the lungs and breathed out. Blood is pumped to the lungs to pick up oxygen and then round the rest of the body by the heart. This beats – contracts or squeezes – between sixty and one hundred times every minute in persons at rest.

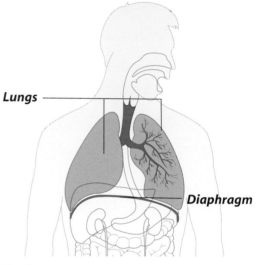

Lungs

Diaphragm

The human respiratory system

Round and round

Four hundred years ago, no one really knew how blood moved inside the body. The most popular idea – dating back thousands of years – was that it went up and down blood vessels, a bit like the tide going in and out. In 1628 all that changed. That was the year William Harvey – physician to King Charles I – showed that blood flows around the body in a closed loop. It travels away from the heart through arteries and back to the heart through veins. Most important of all, he demonstrated this by doing proper experiments instead of guessing, like most other people did then.

William Harvey (1578–1657) proved that the heart pumped blood around the body.

26

How fast is your heart?

You will need a watch with a second hand. Find your pulse by putting two fingers together on the inside of your wrist, just below your thumb. Each pulse represents one beat of your heart. Count the number of pulse beats for ten seconds. Multiply that number by six, and you will get your heart rate in beats per minute. Now run in place for two minutes. Repeat the pulse count. You will discover that your heart is beating faster because your muscles are working harder, and they need more blood to bring them extra food and oxygen.

Did You Know?

How long can you hold your breath? One minute? Perhaps a little more? Dolphins can hold their breath for as long as fifteen minutes while they dive for food. Like us, dolphins are mammals. They get oxygen from the air through blowholes on top of their heads, and they are able to slow down their hearts so that oxygen is pumped around their body more slowly.

Amazing Fact

There are over 60,000 miles (100,000 km) of blood vessels inside you. The main blood vessels that take blood away from the heart are called arteries, and the main blood vessels that carry it back to the heart are called veins. In between, there are lots and lots of tiny blood capillaries in all parts of the body.

Steamy breath

You will need a small hand mirror. Take the mirror and breathe on to it. It will get cloudy, just as the bathroom mirror does when you take a bath because when you breathe out, you are expelling not only carbon dioxide but also small water droplets. These come from the moist insides of your lungs.

Generating Genes

One thing is certain in life: we all have to die sometime. Fortunately, we and our fellow living organisms have a neat replacement service available to make sure someone is there to take over. It's called reproduction. Various ways of producing offspring are used by living creatures. In all cases, the offspring's basic inherited characteristics are determined by genes.

Your genes

Inside every cell in your body is a set of forty-six chromosomes. These are long strings made out of enormous molecules called DNA. In these molecules, a few special groups of atoms occur over and over again in various patterns – like letters in words. If you wrote down a letter for each of these groups in your 46 chromosomes, you would end up with a string of more than 3 billion letters. That's enough to fill 1,000 telephone books that are each 1,000 pages long! Genes are segments of this DNA. Humans have roughly 20,000 to 25,000 of them. These contain all the instructions needed not only to make you look human but also to give you a few unique features.

Whorls and loops

Loop   Arch

Whorl   Composite

You will need an ink pad and a piece of plain paper. The ridges on your fingers are really useful because they help you grip things when you pick them up. You can examine them by making prints of them, called fingerprints. Roll your left thumb on the pad, then roll it on the paper. Repeat with each of your left fingers, and then your right thumb and fingers. Make a note in each case of which finger is which. If you look at each fingerprint you will see it has a pattern. This may be a whorl, a loop, or an arch, or it may be a composite – some mixture of the basic types. All your fingerprints will be different. No two people's fingerprints are the same, not even identical twins (who share exactly the same genes), because fingerprints are not controlled by genes, but by conditions experienced by a baby inside its mother. Your finger markings grow as you grow but their characteristic shape doesn't change.

Animals' markings demonstrate their unique genes.

Did You Know?

Apart from identical twins, everyone has a unique set of genes, so yours are different from those of your parents, your brothers and sisters, and your friends, even if you look or act just like them. The same is true for most animals and some plants. Next time you pass a field of cows or sheep, see if you can tell the difference between each one. It's not always easy!

TRY THIS

Tongue rollers

Collect a group of friends and see how many of them can roll their tongue. Tongue rolling is something that people can either do or not do. There is no halfway. Scientists think the ability to tongue roll – or not – is controlled by genes, which children inherit from their parents. Often, if one parent can roll his or her tongue, the children are also able to do it.

Unraveling DNA

One of the great scientific discoveries of the last century was the structure of DNA. It's discovery meant that scientists could find out exactly how features were passed on from parents to children. By the beginning of the twenty-first century, research had progressed so much that scientists could identify all the DNA making up the genes in human chromosomes. The great breakthrough was made in 1953 by American biochemist James Watson (1928–   ) and English biophysicist Francis Crick (1916–2004). Using information obtained by British chemist Rosalind Franklin (1920–1958) and British biophysicist Maurice Wilkins (1916–2004), they managed to build a model of DNA. It was called a double helix and looked like a twisted ladder.

Growing Up

Whoever you are, your life follows a pattern. For the first twenty years or so you grow and develop, and then growth stops. Other mammals and birds show a similar pattern. Reptiles don't. They grow throughout their lives.

It's just a phase

Growth goes through phases. Human babies grow really fast in the first year of life. In the following years they grow steadily, with their bones getting longer, thicker, and stronger. Then, at some point between the ages of ten and thirteen (earlier in girls than boys), things really start to change. You suddenly get bigger, and your body changes shape so it looks more like a grown-up's. You also start to think differently. This might mean a few arguments with parents. By around age 20, the process is complete, and with luck, the arguments are over.

TRY THIS

Changing height

Use a pencil and a tape measure to measure your height and that of your friends. To do this, find a suitable wall that you can make marks on. (Ask permission first.) Have a friend stand against the wall and mark with the pencil the position of the top of the head on the wall. Repeat this with your other friends, and get someone to do it for you. Do this every month. Are you growing?

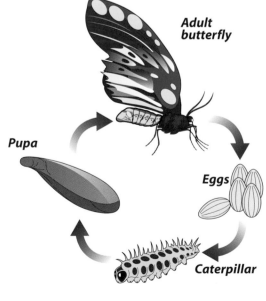

The four stages of butterfly metamorphosis

Did You Know?

Growing up can be more dramatic for insects than it is for humans. The trouble with insects is that their skeleton is on the outside, not the inside. That means that they must "shed" their skeleton every so often, allowing the insects to grow rapidly before their new outer skin hardens. This transformation is called metamorphosis. Some insects, such as butterflies, travel a different route. Their eggs hatch into caterpillars, which crawl around, eating a lot and shedding their skin. Then they rest up for a while as a pupa to reorganize themselves, finally emerging as a beautiful butterfly.

Glossary

bacteria
A group of microscopic organisms that are each made up of one cell

carnivore
An animal that eats only the flesh of animals

cell
The structural unit that makes up all living things

chlorophyll
The substance in plants that makes it possible for them to carry out photosynthesis

classification
The arrangement of something in order or in groups

community
A group of organisms living in the same place

deciduous
Describing plants that shed their leaves every year

decomposer
A type of living thing that breaks down dead matter

digestion
Breaking down food into small particles so it can be absorbed by the body

DNA
The main substance making up living things' genetic material

ecosystem
A community of living things and their surrounding habitat

extinct
Describing a species whose members have all died off

food chain
Animals, plants, and other organisms that are linked together because one eats the other

food web
A number of food chains that are connected

fungi
A group of organisms, such as mushrooms, that do not have chlorophyll and get their food by absorbing nourishment from outside sources

genus
A group of species that share similar features

germination
Growth of a plant from a seed

habitat
The natural living place of an animal or plant

herbivore
An animal that eats only plants

invertebrate
An animal without a backbone, such as insects and worms

mammals
The group of warm-blooded, vertebrate animals, including humans, cats, and dogs

molecule
A basic unit of a substance, consisting of atoms that are linked together

omnivore
An animal that eats both plants and the flesh of animals

organism
A living thing, made up of one or more cells

photosynthesis
The process by which plants use sunlight to make food

reproduction
The process by which new members of an animal or plant species are created

skeleton
The framework that supports an animal's body. In humans and other mammals, it is formed by bones.

species
A group of animals or plants that breed together

vertebrate
An animal with a backbone, such as birds, mammals, and fish

Index